JE NATHANAËL

# JE NATHANAËL

## NATHANAËL

TRANSLATED FROM THE FRENCH
BY THE AUTHOR

WITH AN AFTERWORD
BY ELENA BASILE

Book*hug    Toronto
Nightboat Books    Brooklyn

*Je Nathanaël* was first published by BookThug in 2006.

Design and typesetting by Jay MillAr
Cover design by Kit Schluter

Cataloging-in-publication data is available from the Library of Congress

Nightboat Books
New York
www.nightboat.org

*To Suzanne Hancock*

"These transformations inhabit us."

André Gide did to language an unforgivable thing. He placed it just out of reach. His words are limpid. They are delicate and light. They are as immovable as water, as fragile as breath. Light passes through them. They endure, as he did, the tremors of desire. They transform and enlighten desire. They give voice and take it away. Like a sharp intake of breath upon seeing something startlingly grotesque or unpardonably beautiful. They might have been too much for Nathanaël to bear. So he slipped between or beneath them, and carved his own shadowy way within and outside of that meticulously maintained relationship between desire and language. This is no new thing. Then again. At the close of a belligerent century of calculated tragedy, language suffers still. And the body with it.

What now ? We listen for the echo. We hold it to us and release it again. These transformations inhabit us.

Is there an ethics of desire ? An ethics of language ? Where one begins does the other really end ? Nathanaël is as absent from the pages of his own book as he will ever be. Is that not a great and dangerous thing to aspire to ?

# JE NATHANAËL

*Et parfois je cherchais, par-delà la volupté*
*de la chair, comme une seconde volupté*
*plus cachée.* —A.G.

*My dear Nathanaël I will not write. Every day I take your name into my mouth. I take it and give it away. I would like to inhabit it as you do. Know what it is to belong to no one. Not to exist. Or rather to exist infinitely. I tire of thinking the body differently of searching out the right word for what belongs neither to language nor to silence. You are right not to answer. To go quietly along. As for me I am running and still nothing. I would like to speak to you of the disjointedness between word and speech. Between touch and breath. Skin and flesh. I am a bit like you I don't exist either. If I say : I am I am lying a little bit. Languages hold this way of living against me. I distrust books because of the noise they make. You know how to cultivate silence. I am learning from you. I am learning to be quiet. I am learning to love beside love or the definitions imposed on it. The body leaves itself that's one good thing. At any rate mine does. Nathanaël I did not find you in any book. In any poem. I found you in me. I invited you to dance. We moved similarly. Although distinctly. I sit every day in my garden. Some days I lie in the grass or in the snow depending on the weather. Sometimes it rains. Breath precedes the body Nathanaël. I am breathing differently.*

FIRST BOOK

## THE OTHER BODY

*Je voudrais m'approcher de toi*
*plus encore.* —A.G.

You undress me. Say : A blank. Draw a line. Want me.

Lay me out. Take my hand. Break bones one at a time mine. Sweet dismemberment. By your hand undo me. Broken. I will seek revenge upon your liquid memorial dream soak up your saliva. Your voice on my tongue. Disgorge me.

You said everything about the desert body disappearance. What I know of you a book in the hand. Open myself to the first page. Ardently. I remember nothing neither you nor me. A blank.

I beat you to it. Place your hand on my hip. Say : Read. Blindly.
Roll up the sleeves of my t-shirt you emasculate me (my breasts
stiffen under  your tongue). Slide along my ribs the cold flesh
of your cheek against my bones. Lick fetishist the fold. Sigh :
Beautiful boy. My boy.

     Your fingers travel (rough skin       yes) the length of my
thighs.

I harden in the crease of your ass. Want you. The sea swallows you and me. Say : *Fuck me.* Fucking claims genealogy. Mouths nailed shut. You open. Pronominal. Hold tight. Say : *Hard.*

Fill my pockets with smooth stones. Bind my hands. Say :
Hysteric. Cry out.

Tear out all the leaves. Say : All or Nothing. Knowing full
well that even an empty body has its limits. Run.

Mistake me. Stiffen. Tongue *wet* an injury. What you know :

> The body is a tomb upon which you rest your
> saddened eyes.

> Desire is a chipped fresco.

> Only the hand is capable of translating oblivion
> and transforming it into a gesture.

> A voice is but the echo of shaken bones.

> The blue eye the reflection of the sea.

Fucking. Which way in ? And out ? Book. I tear out all the
pages. Lay you out on your belly. Say open up. I lose myself.

Breathe you in. Mythic. Say : Skeletal.

Tremble. Carry the mark of forgetting. The curve of my
cock.

I haunt you. Polymorphous. Semic. Loiter in closed bars
damp streets unnecessary mornings. Be patient. Yes you. Touch
you hard mouth to back. Raise your ass comes to me.

Ejaculate. You say : Beautiful boy.

Take you multiple divide anatomic this passion. Burst.

You say : Bitch. Forage the ruins so sentimental. Touch the
bottom. I laugh yes.

Say : What a scam. Leave the page illegible. Je. Nathanaël.
Lips bloodied.

Sulk. Implicitly.

In the boudoir primp. Show it.

Push deep. Say : Glutton.

*Lick me.*

You look under the bed. Me. Only me. Seasoned.

What you take I give. A blue boat crosses the blue continent. Milk me. Say : Blue with an *e*. Place your mouth here that I hear you.

Listen.

Hands over and under. Turn around let me see. See. Say : You are crying.

Take a drop on the tongue. Swallow. Bite. Count fingers. Again.

You fall into someone's arms. Rain brings tears. I come.

You say : Not here.

Eyes open I sleep. Night crosses out knocks hard. Temples hammered by no light eyes open sleep. Take my hand. Tongue to palm pull. Fold over and over. I am losing my voice.

Say : Singular. Burst.

You turn on.

Moan. Dip feet into water. Run. Like water I run. Drown. Say : *Ô Capitaine*. Laugh. I fall against you. You against me. Come.

Am adrift. Are.

Betray. You betray the text. I say : The text betrays me.

You turn the page show me despair you are haggard. Kiss me. Hold. Bite neck. Arms outstretched.

You say : Translate me. Find a blade. Slide. Like that. You say : Like that. Sob. Wet. Say : Smooth. Swallow. What you do not know :

Love is running water.

Skin sweats.

Long ago does not exist.

One river's edge is but the opposite of the other. What matters is the water that passes.

A broken voice does not lie.

To each form of idolatry its season.

I love you but not like that.

SCATALOGUE

Books don't show the way but insist on remaining. So how to
leave the book and enter directly into the body ? We are jealous
of one another's bodies yet we each have one. I would undress
my tongue and dip it willingly into ice cold water would invite
you to meet me where the body becomes transparent where
lucidity is a function of the flesh where nothing is for sale and
everything is given away. I would invent rude words for your
mouth show you the true colour of blood. Love in the raw
is life renewed. But of this write nothing down not a thing.
Be wary of the heat that emanates from the unwritten page.
Everything remains to be said so long as we have said nothing.
Most importantly do not fear dirtying yourself. Love washes
the body clean of perfection.

SECOND BOOK

THE VOICE

*Un chien hurlait désolément*
*après la lune.* —A.G.

— Enter.

   I enter.

— Love.

   I love.

— Enter

I enter.

Against me you leave. Here you are. Where I am. You offer a hand. You say : Enter. Which I do. I enter. I sit. I stand. I walk around the room. I run my hand over the walls. I touch. I enter and I touch.

— Enter.

I climb the stairs. Stairs of wood. Stairs of concrete. I climb the stairs and I enter. I go to where you are. Where you wait. What you demand of me. I cross the threshold of the room. I stop in the doorway. I disappear. In the doorway I disappear. Neither shadow nor light. Nothing.

— Enter.

The door is closed. I push against the door. The door resists. I push again. It gives way. I hesitate. There you are and you wait. I look. Nothing. I see nothing. I hear the echo of your voice. Its vibrations in bones. You. Who knock up against my body. Open up. And yet nothing.

— Enter.

Your voice. Your liquid voice. Your seductive voice. Your voice. Your voice which calls me. Your voice which seduces me. Which insists. Enter. Come to me. Your voice which envelops and drowns me. I drown.

I fill my pockets with smooth stones. I fill my pockets with smooth stones and I go to the water. I am drawn to the water. Come. Enter. And I do. I dip my feet in the water. The water licks my ankles. Pulls me in. Come. Enter. And I do. As in a dream. I would have imagined it otherwise. I have imagined it otherwise. The walk toward the end. And yet nothing. I walk. The river swallows me. The river swallows everything. Does not distinguish between one thing and another. Leaves no marks. I am coming to meet you. Me. Come.

— Enter.

You do not come to me. You need not come to me. You are already in me. Enter. And I do. I enter and I do not see you. I sit. I stand. I notice : a window. Still I see nothing. A door. A room. A window. And your voice. Your voice especially.

The window opens onto the street. The street is lit by a street lamp. Obviously. I see the street. The street lamp flickers. The street flickers. Dark street. Wet street. It's raining. I hadn't noticed. It's raining. Cars crease the street. From time to time a car. But mostly that street lamp.

Silence in the room. You say : Enter. I enter. Here I am.

— Here I am.

Nothing. Still nothing.

Not nothing. My voice knocks frantically against the walls of this room. First try : failure. I take note. Failure. I go to the window. I throw my voice out the window. It crumples against the pavement. Nothing terribly impressive. One voice amid so many. I throw it away. I throw it away and I take it back. My voice. I can't decide. I swallow. I puke. Swallow. Puke. The rain comes and washes it away. Washes the street of my puke. Of my thrown-up words. Swallowed again. I say nothing more. My head aches.

— Here I am.

I try again. My voice slides across the floor. Here I am. I leave. Return to the doorway. Here. Where I am. Where I disappear. I introduce a hand into the room. I see it. I see the hand. It remains suspended in the room. I cry out. I don't cry out. My hand. No, not that. Not my hand.

I stop. I look closely. Blue. My hand is blue. Barely but it is. From the doorway. Where I disappear. I look. I look and I see. I no longer hear your voice which says : Enter. Which says : Come. Nor mine which says : Here I am. I say nothing more. I look. I look and I see. I see my hand suspended in a room. I see it blue. I want to leave this place. To run. Fast. But I can't. Not without my hand. The blue hand that is my hand.

I take time to admire it. I have lots of time. At present I have time that I didn't have before. Before. Before what ? What was I doing with my time ? My hand. Here. Where I am. Where I am not.

— Here I am.

Standing on a bridge. I am standing on a bridge. You are not here. You have disappeared. From where you were. The place from which you projected your voice. You are no longer there. You say : Enter. I enter. Say : Here I am. And you are no longer there. So here I am. Standing on a bridge. I straddle a river. Beneath my feet a bridge of concrete and steel connects both river banks. Water runs where you are not. Where the bludgeoned earth runs and water seeps. Here-I-am. Knocking up against the water. Here-I-am. Swallowed up and carried away. I come and I go. From one edge, from the other, I take the bridge. I cross it. Here I am I say. Make myself the echo of my own voice. Yours. Swallowed by the river. With me. Or not. I take my two feet and I leave. I leave the bridge behind me. The water crushes. I touch the bottom. Touch. Here I am. You.

— Enter.

It's too early. Too late maybe. Neither day nor night. Too early. Enter you say. I stay where I am. I do not climb the stairs. Neither those of concrete. Nor those of wood. I do not push open the door. I do not touch the walls. I stay where I am. I fill my pockets with stones. I slide onto the floor. I cross a bridge. Nothing. I do nothing. I do not even wait for you. Certainly I don't hear you. Not before nightfall. Not before the disappearance of the body and the planet. Not before those voices become still, those mouths seek heat other than that offered by daylight, those fingers seek new forms of touch. Only then, yes. Call me. Call me. Come.

— Here I am.

I run to where you are. I run and I lose my breath. I run and I stumble. I fall onto the gravel in front of your place. I skin my hands. I stand up. I continue to run. I run and I say : Here I am. I fall and I do the same. Until I lose my voice. I run to where you are with my bloodied hands. You say : Come. I come but too late. I don't see you.

Want. I want you. Burst into sobs.

— Come.

This is as you announce yourself. Say : Come. I stop. I offer my body. It's too much to bear. I flinch at the sound of your voice. Want it. Again. Come. You touch the bottom. Where I collapse. Where you collapse me. It has come to this. We are on a riverbed. And we are struggling. You. And me. From the bridge I see everything.

Your voice. I sink. I am no longer touching anything. Everything. I would have told everything. To you. Come. I come to you. To where you are not. I find the street. The house is no longer there. Nor the stairs. But your voice. I find the bridge again. Invite the river into me. I run along both edges of the river. Nothing. And you ?

— Come.

I am coming. I travel across cities and continents. I bludgeon the concrete. I hammer against the walls. I take the train, the subway. I pummel the train station. I damn the taxis. Where you are I go. I crumple the ocean. To reach you. Cities and continents. I curse the body, its clumsiness. Fast. Faster. Come. You will not wait. I cry out. I run. I bite my tongue. Bite it again. I am coming. With my bloodied mouth I am coming. My voice hoarsened by the call. Yours. I am coming. I climb up and I climb down. I go where the streets are lit or not. I stand. I sit down. Come. I turn in circles. Where are you ? I crush the city. Your city. I crush it. Come. I am coming. Shame. I am ashamed. Hurry up.

— Enter.

I enter. I climb the stairs. I push open the door. I hesitate in the doorway. I enter.

You pull me to you. Say : Come. I come. You push me against the wall. There. Like that. You say : Like that. I do as you say. The street lamp flickers. Flashes across you. Drowns you in darkness. I see you. I do not see you. You slide onto the floor. Say : Come. I lie across you. You say : Kiss me. I take you into my mouth. I taste you. I cover you in saliva. You say : Yes. You moan. You say nothing more. I ejaculate. You stumble. You sob.

I am where you aren't. I hear a voice. Yours. You say : Come. You say : Enter. One at a time I remove the stones from my pockets. I throw them into the river. I don't even hear the water.

— Enter.

I become you. I become your voice. That distinction. I reach
the last step. I mark a stop. You are not there. I know it already.
Still I open the door. Beat you to it. Here I am. My hand. I have
come to collect my hand. I cross the threshold. I disappear.
The hand appears. There. I knew it. I pounce on it. On the blue
hand. On my hand. It slips away from me. Or rather I miss it.
Whichever. I want it. Give me back that hand. My hand. I run
into one wall then another. I throw myself against the ground.
I run. I run and I run. After that fucking hand. Blue hand. The
street lamp makes the room flicker. Blinds me. I sit with my
back to the window. The light drowns me. Each flicker. Each
flash. Drown me. Fire and water. You are not even there. There
is only your voice which I hold in my hand. The hand that is
no longer mine. I take off my jacket. I decide to stay.

— Come.

I am leaving. I can't take it anymore I am leaving. I take the train the plane my feet. I leave the place where you are not. Here. There. Run. I run. Whatever.

In the desert I build castles of sand that the wind blows apart. Here. There. I disappear. At night I become the desert. I scatter. I scatter my voice. At night I disappear. I follow a trail of moving sands. I make unmake myself. Here as elsewhere. Here where you are not. I walk. I stop. I lie down. I get up. Eyes open or closed I move forward. I am far. Far from you.

And in the very middle of a dune your voice. I wasn't expecting it. In the middle of all this your voice. No. Not your voice. I knock and I knock hard against everything that exists does not exist. I swallow your voice. I shatter into pieces. Your voice grinds into me. I build castles with my bones. I make unmake. You. Open me.

Yours.

— Enter.

I want to know what you see. Say. See. What do you see ? I run my hands across the walls. I close my eyes. Wait. Don't say anything. You take my hand. Say : Touch. I touch. Wait. What I see. You take my hand. Say : Touch. There. Like that. I do not see anything. I see everything. You take my hand. Put it there. The body is hard. Unforgiving. Gives. Takes.

Enter. I enter.

Love. I love.

That's not it at all. The street lamp begins its game. I bite you. Bite. You say : Yes. Again. Bite. Don't bite. I hold my mouth against yours. Breathe in your breath. There. Bite. Wait. Lie against you. You do not move. Moan. Yes. The body gives. Takes.

— Enter.

Your name. I speak your name. Stutter. My fingers dig into your flesh. Syllabic. The echo of my own voice in my mouth. What am I doing ? I am talking to walls now. Your scribbled name. Your stuttered name. Where you are. On the tip of my tongue. You hesitate. Dive. Your name. I speak  your name. You dive deep into me. You swim in me. With your two eyes closed you swim in the echo of my voice. You fear nothing. You lie me down open me. Enter. You enter me. By my mouth my eyes my ass. You lie me down open me. Make me an orifice. I taste of your tongue. Your teeth. Your cadence. You dive drown me.

## A FUCKABLE TEXT

What is a fuckable text and is it only fuckable in English ? Is there such thing as a literary hard-on ? Who wants Nathanaël ? I do I do. Only he doesn't exist. He is not kissing you. He leaves no fold on your mattress. He doesn't break your heart. The tiled floor is cold and your feet are bare. Nathanaël is long gone he was never here not even once. He is a queer boy a loveable boy maybe even a fuckable boy and we are all wet or hard turning pages imagining his breath. You cannot even mourn him because he is not dead. He is not dead because he is not alive. Nobody knows who Nathanaël is. Have you seen him ? I have only seen him from behind in a painting and not a very good one at that. I hear he likes to run in the rain and sleep with his eyes open.

THIRD BOOK

## HESITATIONS

*Dans les trop chaudes nuits de juillet,*
*j'ai dormi complètement nu*
*sous la lune.* —A.G.

The word precedes the body. But which one ?
No use looking.
All books are in need of burning.

The writer has no trajectory.
The body's cartography is shifting.
The voice is but the echo of a voice.
Place is fiction.

Tell me. What do you want anyway ?

Between two words breath.
Between two bodies grief.
Between two cities pain.
Between two voices desire.

Between us the book to leaf through.

Read according to your body's demands.
See everything the eye avoids.
Ask the most obvious question.
Go where I don't go.


Find the border, any one.
Tell me what you see.

To the person who wants to know :

I don't know.



To the one who thinks they know :

Sorry wrong number.

To the other, whom I await :

In the beginning the eye resting upon the hand.
The certainty of not existing.

Afterwards one poem then the next.
You who want to breathe.
The book at your feet.

I tell you this :

Take the door.
Go far empty-handed.
Forget your poems.
Even those that won't leave you.
Do this day after day.

What you pick up I throw away.

DRIFTS

*J'ai bu ; je sais les sources où les lèvres*
*se désaltèrent.* —A.G.

I am a book that has already been written. I am the book no one dares to write.

Who are you Nathanaël ?

FOURTH BOOK

## IN WINTER

*Penses-tu me consoler ainsi ?* —A.G.

Love gives. At the corner of two streets a boy takes me into his arms. He is hard. I feel him against me through his pants. I am shy but I don't stop. I want to invite him into me. When I am sad I think of him. I reinvent him with my fingers. He pulls my face toward his. I would like to touch him but it's cold and my hands are stuffed in the pockets of my jacket. I imagine us in front of a fireplace. I don't know if this is true love but I hope to see him again. We share a beer in a bar. He does not tell me his name. I tell him mine freely. I give. He takes.

I write down whatever I want. What I am not afraid to forget. I keep the rest to myself. Forgetting is necessary. I would like never to know where I'm going.

Wind tears. I don't read anymore. I do a lot of walking. People are looking for me. I don't wait. Today I find myself beautiful. This makes me hard. It's not narcissism. I don't know what it is. I'm hard and I'm beautiful. Everything is possible. The body doesn't lie.

All bodies are guilty of something. All of them. I have decided not to travel any more. Not to dip my feet into the river either. I water the plants. Nobody kisses me. I am a hundred years old.

People think I am mute or even crazy. It's not true. But I'm tired of explaining. I pay particular attention to colours. To the way they bleed into one another.

Words do not come. I sleep on the floor. The mail wakes me everyday. I am waiting to begin.

I see the boy again. It has been a long time. It's noon. The sun stretches into a great gash across the sky. Light spills onto his face. The boy is no longer beautiful. He is a boy among so many others in the street in the middle of the day. What was I looking for ? What did I find in its place ?

Solitudes. I wait for dusk. The western sky split in two. Burst.

Last night I dreamt of a body that was no longer a body. Words bore it no resemblance whatsoever.

FIFTH BOOK

## DESIRE WILL RUN (FROM US)

*...les sources seront où les feront couler
nos désirs.* —A.G.

I said yes. I was caught off guard.

I lost track and left the book open at a blank page. So I followed an altogether different line of thought.

The anxious body undoes itself. Becomes other than the word or gesture that follows closely.

Touch would erase everything. Down to the shiver provoked by a gesture just beginning.


One voice carries another.

The echo is insurgent.

Bones knock together denying the text its impermeability.


As such, the echo carries the fruit of the word's hermaphrodism.

If a word were equivalent to a gesture which obliterates the one that came before, why mark anything down at all, and what could possibly be gained in so doing?

Nathanaël is as silent as ever.

He says nothing. I would like to hear him speak. Or at very least for him to run from or curse the very book he is intended to burn.


It is not possible to love without first being loved. In this way the heart atrophies.

I would like for Nathanaël to be able to die. At least then he will have lived.

The word is enigmatic, especially when mistaken for love and worse still the body.

I want to know what Nathanaël knows without speaking in his place, without interpreting a poem for him, without bullying him, without making him into yet another reflection.

Words are capable of transforming bodies.
This much the tongue knows.

Speak to me of love.

The body opens itself without hesitation to spillages of all kinds, resists being boxed in, becomes familiar with its own tremors, its many sensations, eyes falling where they will, thanks, in part, to gravity.

Nathanaël causes anxiety.

By his absence. By his presence. By his inimitability. As long as he has said nothing, he has said everything. Silence has this ability to render itself limitless.

Nathanaël does not exist. That is his greatest advantage. By his presence, by speaking his own name, he demands the right to passion; he envisions it, commands it, possesses it. Desire comes alive in him.

The anxiety provoked by passion is that very same anxiety which denies the body its own spillage.

To Nathanaël I would lend the following words : 'I am a queer boy.'

He speaks English with a slight accent.

I am a queer boy.

I am learning to read empty handed, to leave room for boredom. I do not want what Gide wants, wanted. Even if from him I learned to want.

Nathanaël surrenders his voice to the body. In this way we cannot hear him. But that is no reason to ignore him. What he does not say he feels.

The tongue trusts in the palate;
The belly in the mouth;
And so on.

By transposing bodies and languages, the species propagates itself differently. I reinvent myself each time you speak to me.

The intrinsic element to this exchange is desire.


Desire
not pornography
nor sadism
nor those harmless illicit affairs.


That universal desire which roots the tree to the earth and tears it from that very hold.

That very impossibility and the conviction that it remains at all times possible.

I entreat you to read eyes closed, to love body open, to break with the organisation of emotions. To stop living beside that greatness the senses offer : unpredictability.


The book is, must be, a call to the senses. There is little else to do than leave it.

The problem with Nathanaël has been presented. It is undeniably a problem of translation. A translation is what is least reliable; one cannot help but resent the text for existing in the first place.

If Nathanaël does not exist, it is because he is waiting to exist. His gestures remain invisible.

The human body is in crisis.

Desire is disappearing.

If I kiss you, it's because I cannot see you. *Wait a minute, that's not what I said.*

Sex is steeped in hermaphrodism.

The translation of the echo.

Language's first defect is its inability to articulate itself. In this sense, Nathanaël is exemplary. He is the means by which we might learn to say everything, if only we learned to be silent.

Touch me. I will disappear.

Listen beside speaking.

If I say I don't read anymore, I am lying.

I am lighting a flame near that which is likely to catch fire.

People are wary of small books, intimate books that slide effortlessly into a pocket. The book's measure is the word. But what of the power of the echo ?

If long ago the word was equivalent to breath and poets were impatient to breathe, today the word is an obstacle to breathing.

We all breathe poorly. The echo dies, see for yourself.

Nathanaël must know this, he who remains silent.

He brings the word back to the body, takes breath into his hands.

What he takes, he gives. The book might be his reward.

We look away from what is familiar, from what is necessarily ugly. We avoid looking too closely, touching. In this way, the book becomes an obstacle, positions itself between me and the experience I might have of the book.

From the lips of Nathanaël, drink.

See.

Thirst does not leave the body.

Gide was not a dupe. He knew that a thing was possible so long as it remained unattempted.


Concert halls are full to capacity.

Stadiums are packed.

Rivers are overflowing.

All the spots are taken.


Nathanaël walks where no one goes.

All quotations appearing in this book are from the inimitable *Les nourritures terrestres* followed by *Les nouvelles nourritures* by André Gide to whom I owe at least a fraction of my literary and sensual antecedence and irreverence.

### A Lie By Its Secret
Nathanaël

*In Art, you see, there is no first person.*
Oscar Wilde to André Gide

The first person may well be the most difficult to translate. If
only because of its insistence on a contestable referent, one
which eludes not only the self by which it comes to be even
falsely identified, but the very language on which it claims
to rest. As far as lies go, it is likely the most magistral of all
for the unequivocal consensus it commands, through a series
of finely wrought lures through which every camel passes,
dumbfounded. And we humans have much to learn from
camels.

*I* stands ever accused, and this is its predisposition. However
much it wills itself, it lacks the full force of being and its
existence is only credible when overlooked. Because it lives by
its secret. And it is a much-abused secret for all the proddings
it must endure into the most delicate folds of its flower. Still,
a flower once divested of its furl can no longer be said to be a
flower. And whatever it has abandoned to posterity it leaves
ostentatiously inscrutable.

An author dies of her book. Each time an other author. And
his names are the eternally precarious signal of a present that
resists endurance. By what fancy then must the present be
called up again and again, to stand the trials by which it is

steadfastly recused? There is much worse than fabrication, there is the tedium which impresses itself in the dusty grooves of discourse.

I have no defense to offer, for the body, or the name. Perhaps it is that the book itself asks to be disabused of its own history and the corrections it seeks to set in place. If it stages its own disappearance through a figure many times imagined, it truly disappears the moment its name is spoken. (Books, too, have names, as do the streets along which they stumble).

To lend credence to the story of the name, however, is to remember a lie and tell it.

I wish only to tell the lie of this book such as it has come upon me. But the lie has been told, and I am it.

January 2018
...
at the reissue
of *Je Nathanaël*
with
and without
its author

**Pressing against tongues.**
**Notes on the name and its ghostly body.**
Elena Basile

*We close our mouths, and we read.*
*When we open them it isn't to speak.*

*Je Nathanaël* is an experiment in prolonged failure: failure of
address in the pronominal intransigence of languages; failure
of desire in its exhausted historical complicity with rigidly
gendered tropes of active and passive; failure of the written
word in its arrogant ascription of bodies to an epistemic
transparency that never was.

Uncompromising in its exploration, the text dwells on the fault
of its failure the way a geologist would dwell on the fault of
fractured rock formations, exploring the veins running through
the uneasy proximity of strata, probing their timeline and the
entangled variables that keep them in place. Or not. Take the
analogy for what it is: an invitation to read the faults of this
writing away from value laden moral negatives, while keeping
firmly in view the gravitational pull of their ethical questioning.

In many ways, the text constitutes its own fault line, spanning
a number of years, versions, and at least two languages,
each exposed to the equivocal proximity otherwise known
as translation. A brief timeline may be of some help here.
Published in French in 2003 and then in English in 2006, the
book's titular character, Nathanaël, makes its first appearance

then as a name that will eventually be adopted as the author's own in 2009. In the present 2018 English edition, such adoption manifests as a doubling of both titular and authorial name, both seemingly converging upon the anchoring deictic force of the first-person pronoun, *je*. It is tempting to read right through that *je* as if its presence alone could bestow autobiographical authenticity upon the doubled proper name against which it leans. Far from having an effect of sanctioning resonance, however, such doubling underscores the book's raison d'être as one of persisting, necessary dissonance.

One can start by noting the intransigent foreignness of the "Je" in the title and by paying heed to the author's own warning in the postface regarding the lie of the "I," its ontological lack and precarious hold on a body it is given to represent, always supplemented by the supposed stability of a self it arguably makes manifest. The proper name, Nathanaël, may be read as supplying such stability, were it not for its intertextual anchoring to the muted addressee of André Gide's *Les Nourritures Terrestres* (1897-1927). Nathanaël may be invoking Gide's Nathanaël across the kind of temporal collapse she is known for having explored in other texts and with other artists, such a Claude Cahun in *Absence Where As*. What I want to note here, however, is the nature of Nathanaël as an *invoked*, rather than *interpellated* name. By this I mean that the proper name gestures towards a body whose conjuring into writing persists beyond and away from "the dusty grooves of discourse"[1] that hegemonic cultural appellations impose.

---

1. Nathanaël, "A Lie By Its Secret", p. 98.

In Gide's proto-queer text, Nathanaël is a "you ... whom I haven't met yet," it is a reader whose "name . . . I give you, ignoring yours to come." Frequently preceded by the vocative Ô across the tapestry of moments of being, which *Les nourritures* could be described as, Nathanaël is the placeholder for a beloved youth figured as disciple, protegé and lastly as 'comrade' enthusiastically encouraged to "throw this book – and go out" after reading.[2] Gide's pre-emptive inscription of a character whose self-possession is pointedly ignored while simultaneously anticipated through the figuration of a body that will wander beyond the book's confines, is echoed in Nathanaël's intensive surrender to a "queer" "lovable" and "fuckable" boy who is "long gone" and yet "cannot be mourned" because he is not dead. And is not *alive*. Such a crepuscular mode of being is of the order of a necessity because Nathanaël belongs to the written page only and exclusively insofar as he *does not*. It is along the tensive faultlines of this mode of (non)being that the text's writing "I" travels.

"My dear Nathanaël, I will not write. Every day I take you into my mouth": the writing body seeks to incorporate the written name—not, however, for the purpose of propitiating ontological plenitude, as if the name (rather than the pronoun, this time) could act as the ultimate guarantor of arrival into the truth of one's own body (a narrative of transition, this latter, which is all too familiar to contemporary readers). On the contrary, the invocation functions as a movement towards disappearance, withdrawal—towards a way of inhabiting the

---

2. Quotations are from André Gide, *Les nourritures terrestres suivi de Les nouvelles Nourritures* (Éditions Gallimard, 1969), p.15 (my translation).

body, which "belongs to no one." If the writing "I" is tired "of thinking the body differently," it is because the language of *thought* is of no relevance here. If anything, what is made clear is that the *languaged thought* of self alone is not only inessential but murderous of a body that it is not for the I to *have* in the first place.

"Languages hold this way of living against me," the writing continues. The sentence does more than gesture to the painful frictions attending to a subjectivity dispersed among more than one language. Beyond that, it gestures to the qualitative dis-placement language as such inevitably operates upon the body. Indeed, however much multiple *versions* of an I may constantly jostle for audience at the threshold of discursive intelligibility (all inevitably consigned to the predictable trends of the day, even the poetic ones), there remains the *matter* of its enfleshment in a body that can only be glimpsed in the fault between "language and silence"—that is, between the opening movement of an address and its echo resonating through a "you" whose answer, or responsive gesture, can neither be predicted nor guaranteed. A you who can slip into the third person (a he, a she, or a multitude of barely individuated they) at whim—the other always hiding among pronouns, stretching them where they can't go, because that's the only path desire leads to. Beyond enticement and beyond the capture of code.

The first two of *Je Nathanaël*'s five books are revealing for how they set up such a structure of address in the form of verbal imperatives in which order and submission, and summoning and appearance, shuttle between an I and a You whose referential consistency is utterly confounded. Who is doing what to whom? Which body wets and which body hardens in the crease of whose ass? Who calls to enter? Who says, "Here I am?" But how many bodies are there, actually? Is there just one, diffracting among sexes? An erotic two? And what about that third, Nathanaël "who was never here, not even once"? To point out the deliberate con-fusion of genders across the pages only tells part of the story. The fact is, each page builds towards its own affective assemblage of bodies none of whose parts adds up to a familiar whole. Nonetheless the reader is given to witness the tremor of each surface, fold or bone sinking into the singularity of encounter. And of flight.

Occasionally the text calls it love. However that may be, it is not the kind that stays put. At the threshold of the sentence, the body stoops to listen for its way out. If Nathanaël is a "problem of translation," as the last pages suggest, it is not because of hermaphrodism or illegibility. It is because bodies persist in their haunting consistency, beside and beyond all languaging intent at capture. But that's the thing with capture: escape is its inevitable corollary. *Je Nathanaël* is there to remind us that breath is always the first to appear. The first to go. Somewhere else, *differently*.

NATHANAËL is the author of more than thirty books written in English or in French, and published in the United States, Québec, and France. Notable works include *Pasolini's Our* (2018), *N'existe* (2017), *L'heure limicole* (2016) and *Absence Where As (Claude Cahun and the Unopened Book)* (2009). Nathanaël's work has been recognized by the Prix Alain-Grandbois, a Publishing Triangle Award, and fellowships from the PEN American Center and the Centre National du Livre de France. She has translated works by Danielle Collobert, Frédérique Guétat-Liviani, Catherine Mavrikakis, Chantal Neveu, and Hilda Hilst (the latter in collaboration with Rachel Gontijo Araújo). Born in Montréal, Nathanaël lives in Chicago.

ELENA BASILE teaches and researches in the areas of cultural theory, sexuality, and translation studies. Her most recent publication on the work of Nathanaël appeared in *Queering Translation/Translating the Queer*, edited by Brian Baer and Klaus Kaindl (Routledge, 2018).

## NIGHTBOAT BOOKS

Nightboat Books, a nonprofit organization, seeks to develop audiences for writers whose work resists convention and transcends boundaries. We publish books rich with poignancy, intelligence, and risk. Please visit nightboat.org to learn more about us and how you can support our future publications.

The following individuals have supported the publication of this book. We thank them for their generosity and commitment to the mission of Nightboat Books:

Elizabeth Motika
Benjamin Taylor

In addition, this book has been made possible, in part, by grants from the New York State Council on the Arts Literature Program and the Topanga Fund, which is dedicated to promoting the arts and literature of California.